GREAT WHALE

Life Cycles

Jason Cooper

Rourke
Publishing LLC
Vero Beach, Florida 32964

www.rourkepublishing.com

PHOTO CREDITS: *Cover, pp. 4, 7, 10, 12, 13, 14, 16, 18, 19, 20, 22 (all photos) © Brandon D. Cole; p. 6 © Melissa Cole; p. 11 © Lynn M. Stone*

Editor: Frank Sloan

Cover and page design by Nicola Stratford

Library of Congress Cataloging-in-Publication Data

Cooper, Jason, 1942-
  Great whale / Jason Cooper.
      p. cm. -- (Life cycles)
Summary: Explores the physical characteristics, life cycle,
reproduction, feeding, and migration of some of the largest species of
whales.
Includes bibliographical references (p.   ).
  ISBN 1-58952-709-7 (hardcover)
  1. Whales--Life cycles--Juvenile literature. [1. Whales.] 1. Title.
II. Series: Cooper, Jason,   1942-   Life cycles.
  QL737.C4C646 2003
  599.5--dc21
                                    2003011553

Printed in the USA

CG/CG

Table of Contents

Although the blue whale is enormous, it can swim at 30 miles (48 kilometers) per hour!

Great Whales

The 10 largest species of whales are commonly called the "great" whales. They are the largest animals on earth. The blue whale, in fact, is the largest animal that ever lived. A blue whale can be more than 100 feet (30 meters) long and weigh 421,800 pounds (190,000 kilograms). That's the weight of 105 large automobiles!

The other nine species (gray, right, bowhead, minke, Bryde's, sei, fin, sperm, and humpback) are smaller than the blue, but they are still huge animals.

The sperm whale, for example, has the largest head and brain of any **mammal**. Its brain weighs up to 20 pounds (9 kg).

A curious gray whale and her baby look at whale watchers in Mexico.

The huge head of the sperm whale is the largest in the animal kingdom.

The bowhead whale is about half the weight of a blue whale. Yet it eats nearly 4,000 pounds (1,800 kg) of food daily when it's feeding. Of course, that's only about half of what a blue whale eats.

Warm air being blown out from the twin blowholes of a humpback whale rises like smoke.

Whales look much like big fish. But whales are mammals, just like us. They are **warm-blooded**. They raise their babies on mother's milk. And also like us, they breathe air. Some whales can remain underwater for more than an hour. Sooner or later, however, whales must swim to the ocean surface and breathe fresh air through the **blowhole** on top of their heads.

A newborn humpback whale calf rests its tail on its mother's back.

From Calf to Adult

A baby whale, or calf, grows inside its mother for several months. A mother humpback whale, for example, carries her calf for nearly a year. In some species, like the gray whale, the calf grows for more than a year before birth. Whales almost never bear twins.

A whale mother pushes her newborn calf to the ocean surface immediately. The calf must have air before it can begin to **nurse**.

The calves of great whales are truly big babies. The largest weigh about 4,500 pounds (2,027 kg) and are about 23 feet (7 m) long.

Sperm whale babies (top and bottom) swim with their mother.

The huge mouth of the humpback whale shows the brush-like plates of baleen.

Whale milk is thick and rich, like a milkshake. Young whales grow quickly on that diet. A blue whale calf, for example, gains 200 pounds (91 kg) per day.

As a young whale grows, it drinks less milk and eats more solid food. Before it is a year old, it stops drinking milk altogether.

The young southern right whale, already 25 feet (8 m) long, is another kind of baleen whale.

Whales eat a variety of food. Surprisingly, huge whales eat mostly tiny creatures. Most kinds of great whales eat tons of animal **plankton**. Animal plankton is a floating stew of small sea creatures.

Whales trap plankton in their **baleen**. Baleen is a set of "plates" in the whales' jaws. As a whale squeezes water through its jaws, "brushes" on the baleen trap plankton. The sperm whale, however, has a mouth full of teeth. It lives largely on squid.

A humpback whale leaps from the sea. The whale wears white barnacles like polka dots.

Whales have few enemies as they grow up. Attacks upon great whales by large sharks or killer whales are few.

Some species of whales, such as the humpback, are old enough to start their own families at four years. Other species may not be old enough to start families until they are nearly 10.

Great whales can live to be quite old. At least one humpback lived into its 70s. Some of the great whales may reach 100.

The Lives of Great Whales

Great whales may be found in large **schools**. That's when the whales are at their feeding grounds or on **migration**. At other times, whales travel alone or in small schools.

A school of humpback whales in Alaska feeds on small fish called herring.

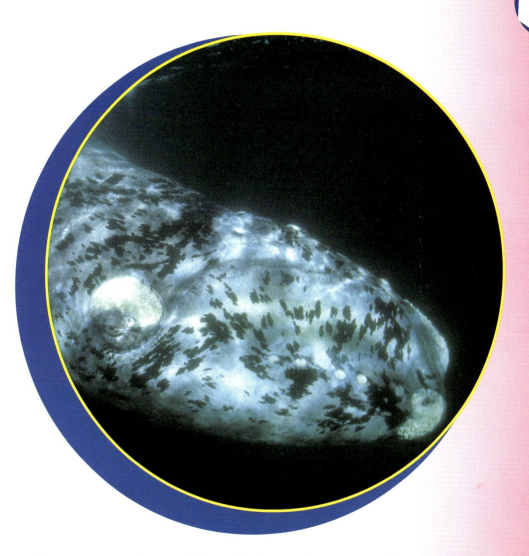

A young southern right whale cruises toward a diver in the whale's warm winter home off Argentina.

Great whales tend to spend warm months feeding in cold waters, even in the icy Antarctic and Arctic oceans.

This young humpback whale will migrate north with its mother in spring from Hawaii to Alaska.

As the air cools, the whales migrate to warmer oceans. There the mother whales give birth, but eat little or nothing. Whales can go for months without eating. They simply take energy from their fat or **blubber**. Blubber is also a blanket for whales. It keeps them warm in the earth's coldest seas.

For many years, people hunted great whales. Today these giants of the seas are protected by almost every nation.

Stage 1:
**A whale calf looks
like a small version
of its mother**

Stage 2:
**A young whale grows up
as it travels with adult
whales**

Stage 3:
**As an adult, a whale
can begin another
whale's life cycle**

Stage 4:
**An adult leaps
out of the water**

Glossary

baleen (buh LEEN) — the tough, comblike plates found in the upper jaws of most great whale species; whalebone

blowhole (BLO HOL) — a nostril in the top of a whale's head

blubber (BLUB er) — fat, especially the fat of whales and seals

mammal (MAM el) — a creature in the group of warm-blooded, milk-producing animals

migration (my GRAY shun) — a long, seasonal journey made at about the same time each year

nurse (NERS) — to feed on mother's milk; to be fed mother's milk

plankton (PLANGK tun) — tiny, floating plants and animals of the sea and other bodies of water

schools (SKOOLZ) — a group of fish or whales traveling or eating together

warm-blooded (WAHRM BLUHD ed) — refers to the two groups of animals, mammals and birds that keep a steady body temperature from within their bodies

Index

Further Reading

Greenberg, Daniel A. *Whales*. Marshall Cavendish, 2001
Kalman, Bobbie. *Whales*. Crabtree Publishing, 2001
Moore, Eva and Sue Rosenthal. *Whales*. Scholastic, 2003
Olien, Becky. *Whales: Giants of the Deep*. Bridgestone Books, 2001

Websites to Visit

www.pacificwhale.org/childrens/
http://www.hsus.org/ace/11739

About the Author

Jason Cooper has written several children's books about a variety of topics for Rourke Publishing, including the recent series *Life Cycles* and *Fighting Forces*. Cooper travels widely to gather information for his books.

FRANKLIN